The
Ambergate
Sonnets

Also by D. J. Etchell

Sonnets from the Iliad
The Lych-Gate
Sonnets from the Odyssey
Not to be read by your Wife and servants

The Ambergate Sonnets

These are the sonnets of a love affair

D. J. Etchell

Burghwallis Books

Copyright © 2012, D. J. Etchell

D. J. Etchell has asserted his right under the Copyright, Designs and Patents Act, 1988, to be identified as the Author of this work.

First published in 2012 by Burghwallis Books

All rights reserved. No part of this publication may be reproduced, stored in a retrieval system, or transmitted, in any form or by any means without the prior written permission of the publisher, nor be otherwise circulated in any form of binding or cover other than that in which it is published and without a similar condition being imposed on the subsequent purchaser.

ISBN 978-0-9560838-5-2

Proofreading, design and dtp by
Mushroom Publishing, Bath UK
mail@mushroompublishing.com

Printed and bound by
Lightning Source

A Dedication
To the only begetter of these ensuing sonnets
B.F.

Foreword

These sonnets have lain in a drawer for over a quarter of a century.

It was my intention never to publish them. Returning to them even now is a source of immense pain and sadness. They were written for someone who I found was my soul-mate. We were exactly on the same wavelength, striking sparks from each other on those infrequent occasions when we met; like twin comets circling within our own universe.

When it all finished, though appearing outwardly calm and cheerful to others, inwardly I was being ripped apart by powerful emotions which were totally beyond my control. These took me to the brink of savage instability, which was made worse by my usual winter depressions. I entered an unreal world seeking any diversion which would take my mind away from my situation.

However, during the last year or so, some other ghosts have been laid to rest; hopefully by getting this last one out of the way I can move on.

I

The golden days of youth were spent and past
Yet deep within us slumbered fires, subdued.
Eyes met, became transfixed and we were lost
As love's soul-searing flame burst forth, renewed.
As comets circling far beyond the stars
Or eddying leaves caught in an autumn stream,
As waves soft-mingling at the harbour bar
We moved as one in destiny's bright beam.
Now, with the hurrying dawn we must depart
As one by one pale stars fade in the sky.
The air hangs heavy, day moves to its start
And lips are met in promise and goodbye.
    Like morning mists which rise above the lake
    The veil of time, for now, conceals our fate.

II

Alone in silence I now contemplate
My love, remote, and in another place.
Parted by life's currents, at the whim of fate;
My memories sustain me as I see her face.
Her lips, her eyes, her languid form, I see
And feel her inward love and longing seek
Past all constraints of life and time, for me;
Thus strengthened I bear out this waiting week.
Then forbidden fires of love we'll feed!
Through hours sweet-stolen, each by each enslaved,
In helpless rapture, aching deep with need
We'll lie long-locked as one, 'til lust's assuaged.
    In lonely meditation, far apart,
        Love smoulders strong, concealed now, in my heart.

III

We met once more and in need's madness loved
Through mid-December, when the nights were long.
I lay with you with all my longings soothed,
Wild ardour dulled by love's sweet siren song.
But shadows lengthen and the daylight fades,
With evening comes the sadness of farewell,
So deep we've drunk the sparkling wine of love,
Yet I must break the rapture of its spell.
As now I speed away through winter's night
My thoughts remain behind, my love, with you
In Ambergate, where I would hold you tight;
Until spring's rebirth helps our love renew.
    Until once more your magic makes me whole,
    Farewell, dark eyed possessor of my soul

IV

Your limbs round mine, the lover's sport we play
Each captive to each other in the night;
We dance to ancient rhythms till the day
To celebrate love's primal, sensual, rite.
Like circling eagles locked in dreaming flight
We soar on passion's currents till the dawn
With wild primeval needs, two, locked so tight
Till, drained, we watch as first light turns to morn.
That languid look: your satyr I become,
Once more compelled to reach ecstatic heights;
My nymph moans softly, waves of pleasure come
As we combine to sample sin's delights.
    If, in love's lists with Venus you must play
    Prepare for toil, till long night turns to day.

V

Now here unmoving, captive to your eyes
Through numbing depth so helplessly I fall;
A silent longing stills my lover's sighs
Another holds you, dancing, at the ball,
And round a stranger's waist now rests my arm,
Her foreign perfume hangs upon the air,
I move within a dream until the dawn
Another's eyes reflect my anguished stare.
You are stood so near and yet so far,
A tantalising walk across the floor;
I curse the circumstances which debar
Me holding you, the goddess I adore.
    On vagrant currents, rudderless, love moves,
    As close yet so remote my mistress proves.

VI

Pensive at midday with thoughts of you,
Alone, and yet not lonely in my rooms,
Your presence in mind's eye will see me through
Until that night when stolen love resumes.
Then in each others arms we'll taste the fruit
Of that forbidden: sweetest taste of all.
The hunted, willing caught in this pursuit,
Perdition risked in answer to love's call.
Outside, dull drizzling clouds blot out the light,
The sun obscured, yet clear my inner eye
Which sees your face far off, a beacon bright,
This lights my day despite this glowering sky.
    In silent meditation in my room
    My thoughts of you dispel this day's dark gloom.

VII

That autumn weekend flew toward its close
And as the day drew on we paused to think
Of others, and in consequence of those,
In sober mood we pulled back from the brink.
We talked things out and thought it best to part,
We took the route we thought would hurt the least
For logic of the mind o'er ruled the heart;
Though hungry still, we early left love's feast.
We parted then and went our separate ways:
Like silent ships, lost, passing in the night.
I wandered then alone through empty days,
Aimless, drifting on the sea of life.
    What fools we were to challenge destiny;
    Those months without you seemed eternity.

VIII

Nine months have passed without you now; I live
Within the raven shadow of despair.
I long for that which only you can give:
Your kiss would lift this curse which I must bear.
Lacklustre life now ebbs through endless days,
Long summer months are wrapped in winter's gloom;
I wither in the absence of your gaze,
Your lips, your wild, wild eyes, your rich perfume.
Life without you is not life, but bleak
Existence on some lightning blasted heath,
Where like poor Lear, alone, I vainly seek
Release, from this black tempest of my grief.
    That promise forged in passion's fiercest flame
        No tears could quench, and cool love's ardent flame.

IX

We did not leave in anger but agreed,
To put aside our feelings and depart.
Poor fools in love to think that *words* had freed
Us from those timeless bonds which bind the heart.
Small pawns upon the board of life we stand;
Inexorable forces shape our fate.
The game of life is not ours to command,
Who throws the dice? Who knows if love awaits?
That parting vow, like mountain snow is melting,
From heights of yearning down the torrent sweeps,
Through its power restraining dams are bursting,
Our love in spate must join us, past that breach.
    We thought our hearts were subject to our minds
    Thus foolishly we parted: love *is* blind.

X

Sheer black silk surrounds your soft white thighs.
You stand in invitation at the door;
Your dress slips down, I watch your nipples rise;
I sweep you up and swiftly cross the floor.
I lay you, ripe, receptive, on the bed,
You arch, invite me, pleading "enter fast".
My blood boils in my veins like molten lead,
Your thighs part wide, then close, as mine they clasp.
Your eyes roll back, you moan as though in pain;
You cry as pleasures' waves crest at their peak.
This agony called love we'll seek again,
But now, full pleasured, spent, we'll drift to sleep.
    Thus, mistress take your lover by surprise:
    Wear sheer black silk around your soft white thighs.

XI

My singing spirit greets the autumn dawn,
With heart light-longing, every moment closer.
By early afternoon I reach the town,
Anticipation mounts, my pulse grows faster.
Through strange streets, my search at last requited.
Your voice rings out, I turn, and then we meet;
Apart so long, so long, yet reunited;
These hours are mine, with you I am complete.
Over coffee now we talk, content,
Just pausing as each others' eyes we seek;
Outside time two lovers gaze, intent;
Spellbound, silent, lost in love, replete.
    No promise made with words could be the same
    As those vows your love drenched eyes proclaim.

XII

Hold me as we gently enter autumn,
As summer's riches start their slow decline.
Gone so soon our youth like spring's first blossom,
Though life is fleeting, always you'll be mine.
Like Augusts' leaves we wait at point of turning,
Exchanging summer's green for autumn gold.
The woods now flame with scarlet garlands burning,
Come hold me love, for soon comes winter's cold.
We, like leaves, must sometime pass forever
Through life's last secret veil on dark winds borne,
Those winds blow chill for you and I must sever,
Come hold me love, I fear the coming storm.
    Suffice this hour, why seek tomorrow's folly?
    Come hold me, end my autumn melancholy!

XIII

There rumours a smile, lingering lightly
Flickering faintly around your red lips.
Eyes closed after loving, mouth open slightly,
Laid on silk pillows in languid eclipse.
Your eyelashes flutter in delicate waking,
Lids open revealing dark indolent eyes,
Your gossamer smile, soft as dawn breaking,
Lights your face gently as slowly you rise.
Modest lids lower, surrendered in greeting;
Soft arms rise open to capture once more,
The feminine essence, tempting, inviting,
Melting, exciting, exuding allure.
    My succubus once more throws wide her gate,
    I enter where forbidden pleasures wait.

XIV

The cup of life, half drunk before we knew
How sweet its taste and yet how brief our time.
Its rim scarce touching lips; then wondering who
Had thieved that nectar pressed from years sublime?
Those carefree days, how could we realise,
We seemed immortal then in endless spring,
Those golden days of youth's lost memories,
Now leave us wise, though sad, remembering:
When we first took the cup and drank so deep!
When fire flowed in our veins and life was free!
Defying fate we took our chance to leap
Into that maelstrom, fate's wild destiny.
    The first young wine is gone but yet the vine
    Still yields a vintage rare, of autumn time.

XV

Each evening's lightening sky releasing
These short day's grip on somnolent woods and fields.
Impatient spring, held, new woken, waiting
Till equinox is past, then waiting yields
And life floods out released from winter's bane,
Brought forth by the song of the waking earth
Which leaps in joy to seek the sun again;
And fertile maiden: spring, swells full in birth.
The cycle turns, the promise is fulfilled
As ordained by some old, eternal, truth.
Time's fleeting essence may not be distilled
We once may taste the heady wine of youth.
    Drink deep of life and love or lose your chance,
      Its golden cup will touch your lips just once.

XVI

Separated by a week; the hours drag out,
An eternity of seven days, so l-o-n-g!
I think of only you in total rout,
In disarray of love, ideas throng
Within mad seething tumults in my brain;
The perfume, shape and sounds of you resound
Smelled and seen and heard, again! again!
Desire conspires my senses to confound.
Yet when we meet tempestuous longings calm,
I take your hands and look into your eyes,
And once again you work your occult charm
And all my pent up yearnings exorcise.
    Till then I wait through seven endless nights
    Each passing second mocks my lover's plight.

XVII

February's meeting caused such pleasure
Yet so much pain. For though we met once more
Love seemed to pause ... and take cold measure
And issue warning that it might withdraw.
All weekend hung that threat of love's demise,
Seen in your face, so full of darkest pain.
I burned in hell each time I met your eyes
Tormented, hurt, yet longing all the same.
Those tortured seconds slowly drifted by
As hour by hour grew worse your hurt and strain,
It chilled my heart to think our love might die
That we would part and never meet again.
    To be so close and have your lips denied
      That lost weekend, fate showed its darker side.

XVIII

Possessed by love, your eyes burn in the night.
Intense desire now twins impelling need;
I claim once more that which is mine by right
As urgently I sate my love's hot greed.
Desire rules all as lips seek waiting lips
Caressing arms now sooth, and urge, and tell
That your forgiveness ends our love's eclipse;
Wild passion's heights will purge our quarrel's hell.
Not until the small hours could we meet,
Now softly in the night your lips reprove
That folly which had caused me to forfeit
One moment of this time we stole for love...
    We fell once more, unable to resist;
    Love's frozen anger, melted by a kiss.

XIX

Now is that quiet time for contemplation
On those deep ways and mysteries of love.
Twice we met as by predestination;
In one sphere our fated stars must move.
Against all odds, drawn by some lure sublime
I came to that first meeting where I found
My dark, wilful, soul-mate, wild, divine.
Though death at last must wishful dreams confound
I'll in these lines your name immortalise.
Forever thus will linger down the years
An echo of that love which linked our lives,
Of anguish and such joy, our hopes and fears
    And thus like Helen's name, or Juliet's
    Forever you will live, in these sonnets.

XX

Mendelssohn, exquisite, hangs in the air,
The violin singing in unrestrained joy;
Beauty abounding beyond all compare
Filled with emotion, love's sweet envoy.
In bright coruscations the notes fill the room,
Sound filling mind's eye with colour and lights,
A pattern hard woven at genius's loom
Forever reminds of our love on those nights.
Now in the small hours half waking I lie
Those sounds and sensations still filling my mind,
Their memory acts as a soft lullaby
Which lets loose sweet dreams of our love, unconfined.
    Until once more I hold you in my arms
    Your siren music binds me with Its charms.

XXI

Blue and deep and empty is the sky,
All is still beneath the midday sun.
A lazy bee meanders slowly by.
Heat-waves rise and shimmeringly run
Along the baked and cracked and thirsty ground,
Which dreams of last night's cool and quenching rain
Of which no single droplet can be found,
No trace of moisture anywhere remains.
Our love once more had gathered like the storm,
Uncontrolled! Exhilarating! Wild!
But separate lives must all desires suborn
And leave needs unfulfilled, unreconciled.
    The storm of longing, just for now, subsides,
    But at its core with you my heart resides.

XXII

Days move slow and life no longer hurries,
House-martins flit and swoop beneath the eaves.
Languid breezes waft away my worries
As on this August day I take my ease.
More than forty summers have I greeted,
Seven winters passing since we met;
Before you life meandered uncompleted,
In slow descent, to emptiness and death.
Yet since we met, my love, my life has purpose,
The darkness which enclosed my soul has gone.
Though youth has fled the best years lie before us,
And we will love until our day is done.
    Though half a lifetime kept apart by fate
    Mature midsummer's love rewards that wait.

XXIII

The bell tolls one and I must leave at last,
Into the night while bidding, soft, farewell.
Though saying 'Go!' your eyes would bind me fast;
I turn away for I must break your spell.
For such allure dwells in those endless deeps,
And such desire for what may never be.
Though I depart, I know your psyche keeps
My soul in chains, you will not let me free.
Now even as I leave you work your art
With soft farewells which echo down the stair,
Words faintly following as I depart,
An incantation in the still night air.
    Sweet sorceress, though ends our love's sojourn,
    Your potent magic binds me to return.

XXIV

Your mocking eyes discern my inmost soul,
Directly reaching deep into my mind.
Now love's perception guides you to your goal;
Unerringly, you know what you will find.
You sensed that I was lost until we met,
As empty as the void between the stars,
Through life's long trance my dreaming spirit slept,
Unnoticed seconds mounting into years.
I looked into your eyes, my slumber broke!
Your lips then, sweetly, helped my soul revive
That shock of love, at last! My slumber broke,
From half a lifetime dead I came alive.
    By chance, beside that lake by candlelight
    You took my hand, our love began that night.

XXV

Summer came a ripening the garden,
Before me hung a fruit so dark and full,
Until that moment I had dwelt in Eden
But for temptation I would be there still.
The curving of your hips gave rise to yearning,
The fullness of your lips awoke desire,
I looked into your eyes and I was burning,
Without a thought I stepped into the fire.
I plucked the fruit and all its pleasures tasted,
In rapture's endless caverns now I dwell,
Just one kiss had all my longings sated
From that moment when in love we fell.
    The garden waits for all to journey through;
    I tasted there forbidden fruit in you.

XXVI

The equinox is past and now comes autumn
Swollen, juicy, damsons bend the bough;
Leaves are falling, paying winter's ransom
And with that carpet golden woods endow
With ripe sepulchral colours of decay.
Fevered reds combine with ancient yellows
Palsied greens meld with the feet churned clay
Plucked by wailing winds they join their fellows;
Then sere and silent, laid in vast array,
They await that final transmutation
To elementals, freed from death's dark sway.
Above, the buds await reincarnation.
    'Mid agonies of beauty we decline,
        Our lives like leaves soon swept away by time.

XXVII

Sultry summer's days at last have ended
Martins' nests are empty, young have flown,
Into the mists once more our year has wended,
As autumn leaves love's memories are strown.
Plaintively our last farewells are sounding
Like pagan pipes which in the distance call
A last lament, so mournfully reminding
That love has briefest season of them all.
Now dulls our rapture with the year's last ember
And fades your lips' red promise as the rose,
Our ardour must decline as sad September
Brings this perfect season to its close.
    Would such a summer's passion come again,
    This evocation, hopelessly, I pen.

XXVIII

Dank hangs the fog, unmoving in the air,
Enshrouding trees and causing them to shun
These pillared vaults, through which in dark despair,
Slowly falls the trillionth leaf of autumn.
Condensing mist runs dripping from the bough
Upon the sodden carpet of the earth.
Spring's rich green mantle all has vanished now,
The wood stands bleak, cathedral bare, in death.
My steps are muffled as they, listless, fall
Upon this rotting layer of black decay,
For life has fled from nature's sumptuous hall
And summer's golden days seem far away.
    I stand like sombre winter, dead and drear
    Devoid of love, depressed, at my nadir.

XXIX

Dissatisfaction fills my brooding mind
At that which we would wish, which cannot be;
The burden of its longing, dark confined,
'Til death's transmuting kiss can set us free.
My being's essence wishing for release
Must serve its term within this fleshy cage
Until time turns the key to give release
From long despair in life's remorseless rage.
Without you, trapped by fate which seeming mocks
Our little lives and schemes through empty days,
Infected by desire which like some nox-
ious fever, acts to deepen my malaise.
    Love's darker moods conspire, I know too well,
    To turn our latest parting into hell.

XXX

I drove once more past dreaming Ambergate
Oh! What memories lie sleeping there.
That name I ever must associate
With you! Romance still permeates the air,
Which cloaks that quiet vale in which we met
All burning summer long, Oh! What hurting
Was confessed for we incurred that lover's debt,
Its forfeit paid, the price was that of parting.
I slow and glance across the hill. The white
Stone house stands waiting still, for our return:
We never will! Nothing ever can requite
Those kisses on lost nights for which I yearn.
    I turn and look; the moment slips from view,
    Receding now with Ambergate and you.

XXXI

In the small and silent hours we talked
And spoke of last goodbyes, polite, controlled;
And yet we nearly broke as yearning stalked
The shadows there and threatened to take hold.
We held the urges back which welled so strong,
Inside we rationalised and then, morose,
Prepared to part; yet kept in check so long,
Emotion gained release as we held close,
Locked lingering in a last embrace ...*that look,*
Led to a desperate kiss, love's demon
Had us then, and all that I'd forsook
Your lips reclaimed and what was lost was won.
    Surrender led to such a night aflame,
        Our love consumed us till the dawn light came.

XXXII

Was it six or seven? I left your room
And stepped into that light, where morning's grey
Unmoving mist unites with Sunday's gloom;
Low silences filled empty paths as I sped on my way.
Yet in that stillness I could scarce contain,
My joy, as I strode lightly through the park,
Recalling sin, such pleasuring, which came
As we lay close, enfolded by the dark.
The phoenix fires had dimmed and thus required
A spark sublime, to spring once more to life.
Your drooping lids surrendering, conspired,
Provoked desire which raged through all the night.
    Behind me cloaked by morning's soft disguise
    Is hidden: love's inferno, in your eyes.

XXXIII

A very purposeful figure strides
To claim what she desires, her dark eyes burn
As blood hot lust comes flooding in red tides.
To flee is not an answer! I may not turn
And run: I know I would be hunted down –
The danger grows with every stride as this
Wilful female, a temptress of renown,
Now takes her prey — your pardon while we kiss.
With iron determination she leads me
To her lair, leaving me in little doubt
What fate awaits me there. Let this tale be
Warning! There is just no way out!
    I am master really, I must make that clear.
    Excuse me I am needed, again! At once my dear.

XXXIV

And now we sit, alone once more, among
These stolen hours. We talk of happiness
And think of all those wasted years, which throng
The night as memories: old ghosts which press
As haunted shadows here. You know my love
How long we've searched, yet found no remedy.
Now as hot beauty wells, then spills, you prove
What price is paid, in helpless misery.
Yet I would take you in my arms and fold
You in my dreams, and melt the pain which fills
Your eyes to halt those hard cried tears. To
Hold you for a moment suffices come what will.
    Apart we yearn, tonight we burn within
    Till time or fate can end love's suffering.

XXXV

So now you sit upon the eve of forty,
With mocking dread you wait the midnight hour.
Have your years been full or, aching, empty?
Has life been sweet or has its taste been sour.
I think, despite your heartache, not the latter,
A spirit such as yours would overcome:
Regrets and doubts, snares which the fates would scatter,
To subdue those, who lacking fire, succumb.
Locked deep within you I have felt a yearning,
Desire and love and courage fierce aflame,
So rare this beauty born of life and loving,
Which by this verse I tenderly acclaim.
    We met beside a lake by candlelight,
      There in my dreams you fill my arms tonight.

XXXVI

We made love and then again, again, and
Then once more. I tried to leave, you bade me
Go, I reached out for the door. Now understand,
I tried but found I could not turn the key.
So feminine your rounded form, hot, lewd—
Reclined, so meltingly lascivious.
Your heavy languid lids conspired, renewed
Desire, thus we resumed, oblivious
To approaching dawn now sneaking stealthily
To steal love from us. Thus with lust curbed
I must depart, the stairs so quietly
To climb, to dream in silence undisturbed.
    Of secret love's past splendour now I write,
    When we were spent, in wantoning the night.

XXXVII

So close, so close and yet constrained, by eyes
Which seek that furtive touch: to tell,
That we are lovers, of the night. Your sighs
Of silence scream my name so deafeningly well.
The music drones, they come and go, and now
The party's at its height, the cake is cut
And champagne flows, their laughter, hollow,
Mocks our plight. Feigning boredom, eyes half shut,
I dare not seem alive near you, for once
My mask of caution dropped to give desire
Its rein, your merest gesture in response
To set love free, is all I would require.
    The night slips by, I sit as in a trance,
    Your willing lips denied by this mischance.

XXXVIII

With passing time what glories fade away,
The joys of strength and quickness of the mind;
These laurels of our prime must all decay,
With lives to dust and history consigned.
So soon are gone those reckless days of youth,
That gift most precious, valued least, until
We realise at last that fateful truth:
That all too soon we are forever still!
Yet for the moment we will drink so deep,
Of love, until its fountain falters, dry.
For fate has sown but let our passions reap
The harvest of our meetings you and I.
    In your soft arms I live a thousand lives,
      Deaths embrace, far off, forgotten lies.

XXXIX

Cast through space by a boiling cauldron's mass,
Diluted by distance and atmosphere,
Light cascades and warms with its caress,
My supine form, within the garden here.
Oiled and bronzing I luxuriate,
Carefree, cooling in the gentle breeze,
I think of you and idly meditate,
Lost in fond reverie beneath old trees.
Oaks rustle, unnoticed, at my left side,
I vacantly gaze at anemones,
Unseen are the swifts which above me glide
As I drift now with you amid memories.
    My dreams float above, with the cumuli
    As I dream of that lake where we met, you and I.

XL

Dotted here and there a yellow neon glow
As feeble street lights challenge days last light.
Below the skyline squats my empty bungalow,
Surrounding trees stand black as hell's midnight.
Haloed by the afterglow of sunset
As turquoise shades transmute to velvet blue,
Where this longest day has briefest night met,
In its perfect stillness how I want you.
Your absence mars the beauty of the evening,
An emptiness of longing fills the night.
Yet now, above, the stars grow brighter, pointing,
To where the flame of love lies, burning bright.
    Midsummer's eve eleven twenty five,
        The brooding dark descends, I turn and leave.

XLI

In that last sleep from which we never wake
A dark infinitude must claim my soul.
Faith or reason can no difference make,
For death must win the strongest of us all.
In love's light lies, we briefly seek relief
Or reach for fame's illusion in our hour,
A kiss is sweet, the taste of glory brief;
Drink deep for endless night comes ever near.
Yet while I live your perfume I must breath
And drink of love's sweet nectar at your lips,
Thus for a moment fate's edict deceive
And in your eyes elude life's last eclipse.
    We seek beyond our time-leased lives in vain,
    Our love alone redeems tomorrow's claim.

XLII

Once in a lifetime fortune's smile might beam
On those, unsatisfied, compelled to seek
For meaning in this chaos clouded scheme
Of things, and by illumination wreak
Some small revenge upon the mocking gods.
For others death comes soon and perhaps most blessed
Are those who early leave the stage — to clods
Who slowly find indignity in age, before their rest.
But best of all is love; for those who taste
That cup divine, burn with celestial fire.
They gain that prize, denied to those who waste
Life's chances chasing counterfeit desires.
    I riddle here, love carnal or divine?
    I hold the cup, you know who pours the wine.

XLIII

You phoned me and the date is set to meet,
Where I had thought was vanished and long past.
A place where lovers met and bitter sweet
The game was played and where our lips touched last.
Ambergate, the music of that name
An ordinary place but haunted yet
By those who loved, whom love drove half insane.
There we parted but could not forget,
That summer's stolen meetings and that name.
Tomorrow waits the journey to your arms
Once more to lose my soul deep in your eyes,
The spell is cast, you lure me with your charms,
Now I must wait to find what fate contrives.
    Can longing mend our late love's broken vow?
    Or is that summer lost forever now?

XLIV

You drove in slowly, smiled, as there I stood,
Legs weak, for you were close enough to hold;
Desire repressed so long became a flood
As you at last within my arms I fold.
The urgency of need stayed unexpressed,
Yet wildness of desire burned deep within,
A touching of our lips, no words were said,
A look sufficed, delayed for now was sin.
I smelled your perfume, drank your presence deep,
Your scent and those of summer intertwined,
Your eyes invite, intoxicating, sweet,
Within those depths waits pleasure unconfined.
    All needed, there, decreed again by fate,
    A warming breeze and you in Ambergate.

XLV

The rich bequest of summer's lazy days
Once more fulfils the promise of the year,
For weighted now with fruit each vine displays
A bounty, which must always disappear.
With lengthening nights hard winds must claim their toll
And early frosts spoil fruit upon the bough,
For autumn comes, with mists, decay and dole:
The umber months must have their season now.
We too from summer's plenty must descend,
Despair and desolation fill the mind;
Now as the year declines towards its end
Our love once more to winter is consigned.
    Our meetings are past-poignant memory,
    Love's rapture is the dust of history.

XLVI

My candle gutters in the vault of time
Its light consumed by that immensity;
A feeble flicker which will soon decline,
Consigned to nothingness by destiny.
The winds of autumn promise winter soon,
Where barren fields and empty branches mourn
Beneath the ghost light of the harvest moon;
My twin in solitude, alone, forlorn.
The amber desk light casts a sombre glow,
My pen stops moving as I think of you.
A premonition, dark, disturbs me now,
I doubt if spring will let our love renew.
    These months without you, filled with ennui.
    Now, melancholy has the best of me.

XLVII

Should youth return and ask, impromptu, where
The years had gone and mock at middle age,
What would you reply? Would you despair
And wish your time again? To drink, assuage
Your thirst once more with folly, as of old,
Or perhaps revive the appetites of pride
And try once more to comet through the world,
With youthful, brash, impatience as your guide.
Or would you, having love within your reach
Be content that now to memory confined,
Those former madcap cavortings will teach
How richer passions sate the mature mind.
    I know well where the greater pleasure lies,
       For such contented beauty fills your eyes.

XLVIII

Waiting for your phone call, for the voice which
Will revive me; restoring zest for living
At the turning of the year. I feel such
Apprehension at this seasons passing,
Soft shadows fall in mourning now that autumn
Days are here. Leaves fall in the forest
And tides of life seem ebbing, the sun
Sinks ever paler, weary, to its rest.
These days now seem to shorten, in prelude to that
Wakening, which heralds spring's, wild coming.
Now love dons winter's cloak and sere cravat
And I must wait to see what March will bring.
    I burn and fret, by each long second cursed,
        One word from you, my mood Is soon reversed.

XLIX

Secretive, guardedly, now each word,
Wary and watchful we spoke, whispering
Most carefully, so not to be overheard.
Yet sensuous grew your murmuring
As I recalled desire, and what we did
And how you looked consumed by passion's fire.
Please don't, you moaned, as you that night relived!
Then languidly, much later, with mischief you enquire:
Did I remember too? The tables turned!
Could I forget that pleasure's hell in which
We'd loved that night; recalling it I burned.
With subtle skill your words once more bewitch.
    For though I played in pleasuring you then,
        My complement returned in sweet revenge.

L

The latest of my sonnets will not come
As far too long now we have been apart;
The fires of love need fuel to consume
And keep its flame alive within my heart.
Each day drags longer than its summer's mate,
Each hour hangs heavy in the winter's gloom,
Each second questions: how long must I wait?
Until love's conflagration can resume.
The fire I need burns hot within your eyes,
I seek its love glow blushing at your cheek,
The furnace waits, yet destiny denies,
Our chance to fuse once more in passion's heat.
    Desire is starved through winter's freezing night,
      Love's conflagration waits till spring's fresh light.

LI

I stand before you at the eventide,
A moment stolen once again from time,
I hear the heartbeat of your pained love chide:
How long, how long your lips were kept from mine.
I drink the music of your presence deep,
My psyche soaring in love's ecstasy,
For many search but very few will reach
That goal which love may steal from destiny.
Once more I hold you tight and that is all
I ask, this is where I long to be.
Beyond all reason I must heed your call,
And come to you through all eternity.
    Now winter's darkness all our world consumes,
    Spring must wake before our love resumes.

LII

A sense of the pagan fills my mind
As idly down tree shaded paths I muse,
Here furtive shadows flicker as the wind
Disturbs dry leaves, aflame with autumn's hues.
Often down these hidden ways past lovers
Met and kissed—soft lips, strong vows, long done,
All vanished now, and restful earth avers:
Love whilst you may, for soon you lie alone.
Many such as I have passed this way and sought
For answers to life's trials, and longed and wondered.
Of instinct deep within is born this thought:
To love is all, love's power lives unended.
    Will those who follow this same question ask?
    And dream these dreams, before they onwards pass.

LIII

Once more this strange sensation overcomes
My senses as I feel the start of spring
Approaching fast. Such urgency now runs
Abroad as life begins its wakening.
Melting snow withdraws its winter blanket,
The snowdrop and the crocus show their blooms,
Soon Easter, then the daffodils' bright carpet,
The equinox must pass, then love resumes.
The cycle is eternal, we are mortal,
Our moment short-lived on the sands of time.
Before we stand before that last dark portal,
Embrace once more this season and be mine.
    Hurrying, hurrying, life cannot wait!
    Like spring's fragile blossoms love can't hesitate.

LIV

To rapture's mad maelstrom once more we're drawn,
That tempest: compulsion, sweeps over us now.
Once more in love's tumult must logic drown,
For lost in lust's vortex, helpless, I vow:
That this time there will be no farewells,
No lips that slow linger before we depart,
No eyes moist through heartache as fate's writ compels:
That goodbye, which once more will tear us apart.
But hope cannot alter what two lovers know!
Desire cannot change where our destiny lies!
Our paths, pre-ordained, wait immutable now,
For the mind must accept what the heart denies.
    Love fast consumed those brief, sweet nights we met,
    I long for those which wait to claim us yet.

LV

Time is the enemy! Ungraspable!
Slyly stealing ever mounting seconds
From our lives. Elusive and invisible,
Like dew drops in sunlight, each fast absconds.
Almost unnoticed, all these tiny legions.
These motes decamp, a never ending stream,
Sad moments which must eat away love's season.
Thus, inch by inch we die. For life's sad dream,
That miser of our hours so little has allowed,
Disjointed moments snatched from wasted years.
Yet to its mocking goad such ecstasy is owed
And hope lives on beyond all parting fears.
    The sands of time run slow when you are gone
    At your return they linger, fevered long.

LVI

Dull love in sloth and slumber has declined
Through green decked spring, now burgeoning sublime,
So sure that as May ends, bright June will find
From flower's first swellings on the sap filled vine,
Dark waxy, tiro, pea sized plums, in green.
Thumb-nail, hairy, apples drip fresh dew
As Cox and Russet drink the sun's bright beam,
But now I languish lost and far from you.
This season's darkness clouds my brooding soul,
I know that summer's brightness will be veiled
As clouds of anger rise beyond control,
The harvest of our love it seems has failed.
    My mistress now from me I fear has fled
    And all fond hopes lie lifeless, withered, dead.

LVII

Impromptu thoughts this blackest time displace.
I think of you with fond dark impotence,
Then I am lost in reverie's vast waste,
A desert world devoid of love, immense.
Around me life resumes its stolid flow,
But thoughts of you overwhelm me now,
Thus, my sense of emptiness must grow
As I endure your enforced loss somehow.
I start, and wake, the sadness comes, I sink
Beneath self pity's waves, its ebbing current
Strongly runs and carries you from mind; ink
Drying slow is signed love's malcontent.
    Past thoughts of you such painful times recall,
    Recorded in this brooding sonnet's scrawl.

LVIII

Slowly now our farewell's pain subsides,
Our passion's torrent lost within the mind;
Finally its last lost ripple chides,
Retreating from that maelstrom left behind.
It seems I live, a dreamer on the shore,
Who waits forever for the turning tide,
Love's ocean ebbs for me now evermore,
And carries you beyond lost hope's divide.
I wait, an empty vessel on the sand,
Beached and battered by love's raging seas
A derelict decaying on life's strand,
A bleaching hulk of haunted memories.
    The tempest: pleasure, waits, far off, sublime.
    Whilst I bound in love's doldrums fret and pine.

LIX

Driving north, the harsh sky's last pale streak!
An angry scar! Now fading as descending
Dusk devours the light. My mind runs – bleak
Before the storm which mirrors my remembering.
Where from here my love my love? These break-heart
Meetings mock our fate, the lie we live
Conspires to keep us far, so far, apart:
Days tantalise, by taking what they give!
Lost hours, once more in Ambergate we met
Upon that yearned for summer's eve, unspoken
Longing filled your eyes with such heartfelt regret,
Then lips exchanged one last sweet lingering token.
    Though love's delights and agonies combine
        I live for those brief moments when you're mine.

LX

Exactly as a year ago, in fading light
I think of you, where waking
Street lights cast their glow, diluting early night.
The breeze blows wistful on my brow, caressing
Sorrowed thoughts of you, through seasons four
The earth has turned and nothing is resolved.
Time passes drawn by some remorseful law.
Perhaps all must end before I am absolved.
I ponder on love's destiny,
What pain through future years is strown?
I drift with vagrant memory,
Forever now it seems I am alone.
    Past pleasures tasted in your arms are gone,
    Time's mocking finger beckons; I walk on.

LXI

A perfect summer, sadly, now is dying,
Its shroud of mists and shadows veils the trees,
In autumn's arms fond memories are lying
Of sun-kissed glory, gathered like the sheaves.
Wild gold has vanished from the sheltered valley,
Sparse ranks of stubble march across the field;
Leaves grow yellow, failing, yet they dally,
Life's dregs are sweet beside those death might yield.
Reluctantly, we too must soon relinquish
Those heights we scaled when in our godlike prime,
Nights grow longer, soon lost years will vanquish
All hope, all love, all reason for all time.
    Fate alone must know, yet gives no reason,
    Why dark corruption ends perfection's season.

LXII

Despite my need and your desire I play
The waiting game. Passion's greed will take its toll,
You must be mine, whatever you now say;
I know the signs; I watch you lose control!
Seductive moonlight fills the room, your sighs
So softly shriek for what must be,
For helpless flesh must give what will denies!
As you succumb to needful ecstasy.
Suddenly you melt and change, lips open
Wide with mad desire, instinct has possessed
Entire; the chains of your denial lie broken,
And frantic longing is by love expressed.
    Temptation's cup is proffered, you are mine
      Your harsh denial repaid by hours divine.

LXIII

Through inky vastness heavens extend:
Infinity, through time stretched far above
Until lost star flung photons end,
In eyes which gaze where ancient comets rove.
Eternal, perfect, beauty haunts the night,
Returning moonlight brings its mystery,
Lovers, spellbound by its power, locked tight
Within each others arms, taste ecstasy.
I am chained though in this world below,
And know that dreams must die, unrealised,
Within life's vault, so briefly ours to know,
Before we join those legions death has scythed.
    Life is empty, blind fate casts cruel dice,
    Can love torn from its vagaries suffice?

LXIV

The beauty of soft morning mists in autumn
Drifts, silent, through the hollow near the stream,
As though this season hangs a flimsy curtain
Around that change which ends midsummer's dream.
Love's promise is so fickle, brief, and fleeting,
Lust's sweetest kisses, bitterness conceals,
Undying ardour vowed at lover's meetings
Must fade with time, which ever deathward steals.
Yet you are constant as the stars of evening
Or dawn which lights my room with its soft glow,
What flames deep in your eyes is undeceiving:
Love's undiminished need, my heart should know.
    The transience of life's short span, so strange,
    Weighs on me, yet I know you cannot change.

LXV

With autumn days once more come thoughts of death
As on the evening mists is smelled decay,
Exhaled from mouldering leaves, a final breath,
Before they join earth's shroud, becoming clay.
Now is the time for silent owls to swoop,
Abducting bright eyed, fat, unwary voles,
When beetles march and dark gilled fungi droop,
Releasing spores which drift through wooded knolls.
For days grow short, brief lives must falter soon,
All love, all hope, all mortal things must cease,
Life seems pointless in this lengthening gloom,
Cursed days need spring and you to bring release.
    I'm weighed down by this dark season's pain,
      Dejection, decline and corruption reign.

LXVI

The winds of life like those of autumn change,
From settled days soon icy tempests run,
This mirrors human love, so fickle, strange,
From bliss filled nights is raging heartache won.
Inconstant roar love's surging swirling tides,
From mountain heights descends its passion's storm
To silent deeps, where spent desire resides,
Couched in slumber till the dreaming dawn.
I seek the tempest, crave the raging seas,
Abhor those empty doldrums where I yearn
For your soft breath which wakens longing's breeze
To drive that storm of lust in which I burn.
    Tranquillity can wait the life beyond,
    Wild elementals call, I must respond.

LXVII

I sit with vacant eye and lift the cup
And wonder how much longer now before
You will arrive; the minutes pass, I look
Around with absent mind, then lift the pot and pour.
Then suddenly you have appeared and stand
Beside the door, as our eyes meet your smile
Reveals love's secret things which now demand,
That I must come and serve you for a while.
I think about this challenge you present!
Erotic tension fills the air, we chat,
Excitement mounts, your clear intent
It seems must lead to something at your flat!
    Hand in hand into the night, palms tingle
    Suspense and hot desire now intermingle.

LXVIII

I sense that you can hardly wait as now alone
With breathless voice you ask me coyly
What I would have done if I had known,
With unashamed wantonness you taunt me;
Explaining in that place with crowds around
That you had on beneath your soft draped dress,
Besides grey nylons, as I later found;
Suspenders too, you played with me temptress:
Nothing else! Aroused, I acted, seeking
To find out just what your words implied!
I must leave you now my reader hot imagining
What then transpired, were love's needs satisfied?
    Love long denied your stratagem condones,
    My payment rich, in harvesting your moans.

LXIX

Such is its nature, parting's gloom comes down
To crowd with bleak depression my black soul,
From height of heights into that abyss thrown
Yet in those despair's depths new dreams console.
My absence from you melancholy brings.
I know that past and future time must meet,
Yet mournful fate's slow pendulum now swings
As barren nights, with bleakest days compete.
I hear your voice as wind blows in my eaves,
Your tears fill squalls which blast my window pane,
Your ghostly sighs which moan amid the trees
Will haunt me 'til your soft lips I regain.
    From each farewell must love's next meeting follow
    Yet with your absence empty words ring hollow.

LXX

Golden October, Sunday afternoon,
Summer's haunting beauty lingers still,
As warm sun bathes dry banks where all too soon
Blown leaves will mass to choke the winding rill.
Now by the copse the slow plough brows the earth,
Surrounding hedge hung fruits droop, over-ripe.
All must eat their fill for soon comes dearth
As empty winter clothes the word in night.
Though now the gorgeous autumn halls are full,
How soon to bleakness must our days descend?
Fulfilled in purpose all must turn and fall,
Like leaves our love's brief season too must end.
    I dream of you where woods and hedgerows burn
    With fruits lush as those lips for which I yearn.

LXXI

Now summer's end has come, the swifts are massed,
Swirling, whirling, soon they sunwards soar;
Then vanishes a season unsurpassed
As dying days slip off through autumn's door.
Soon harsh November brings its gales and frost,
December's gloom and sadness next will fall,
The solstice looms, when all the world seems lost;
In winter's crypt spring wait's the sun's recall.
These years are few which circumscribe our lives
In which we find so little can we know,
Yet beauty moves, hope lives, and love inspires
Before we into endless darkness go.
    Long in the vault of time past seasons lie,
      There fate will lay lost dreams of you and I.

LXXII

Blood pinks with weeping greys now usher night,
Weird storm dragons ride the western sky,
The earth grows barren with dark winter's blight,
Proserpine, in slumber long must lie.
Our planet rolls inexorably on,
Unnumbered seasons wait to take their turn,
The world is dying, paler grows the sun,
How weakly now love's embers feebly burn.
The pagan in me fears the fading light
And yet I know that summer must renew
That beauty which is banished from my sight,
Those lips and arms and eyes announcing you.
    Now is the time when love with winter dies
    This weary season all my hope denies.

LXXIII

Bright stars the velvet night's diamond, the Moon
Has beauty old, the sun runs its eternal maze
Above love's sacred grove. We part so soon,
Yet fate leads on through old infernal ways.
The game is rigged she throws the dice;
I drink the wine and pay the price: my soul
My all; a fool asks why love's sacrifice,
Sweet kisses bought by agonies so cruel.
One touch of your burning lips, there at once I fell,
The cup was offered full, I drank
And tasted Heaven and Hell,
As to love's heights then to its depths I sank.
    Though all our worlds at last to dust descend
    Vicissitudes of love will never end.

LXXIV

Samhain, November, and the old madness
Envelopes me, I pick the last Russet
Brooding down dark lanes, where autumn's sadness
Shrouds the drooping trees at sombre sunset.
The woods, aflame, are dying once again!
Unbearable, this beauty of decline!
I know that life can never be the same,
The chance is past which could have made you mine!
What point has life, so empty and insane?
My shrouded spirit seeks solace and peace,
For powers of darkness rule until Beltane.
Goodbye for now, can spring bring my release?
    The apple core, discarded, whirls down stream
      Like futile love thoughts, vanished is my dream.

LXXV

The early mist hangs dank and chill, and brooding
Black stand winter's trees in mourning.
Long shadows, dark and still, fall, shrouding
This sad funeral shortest day now dawning.
The grave yawns for a year, near dead, whose passage
Leaves no mark on time; what's done is done,
We drank love dry, yet failed to assuage
That thirst sublime, which torments hours alone.
Grey spectral clouds hang low and dull like care
Which crowds my spirit so; the year will turn
And hope may come, but now I ask: oh where
Are you! Where are those lips for which I burn?
    Depression damned, I curse the brooding dawn
    Lost days of darkness follow nights forlorn.

LXXVI

Now is bleak winter's time when nature mourns
And overwhelming night consumes the day.
Long shadows haunt me, January comes;
That charnel month of sadness and decay.
Now is the sombre season. Unexplained
Depression hangs above my world, the curse
Returns once more. My spirit ebbs, with nothing gained
From time but empty disillusioned verse.
A new year starts and in my heart I know
That all things must renew and love returns.
Thus as spring comes my joy for life will grow,
Till once again I hold you in my arms.
    Another year has come and gone and we,
    Poor pawns of fate, await our destiny.

LXXVII

We groan through twenty, thirty thousand days,
Time sucks us dry and then discards the shell;
We tread where better feet have worn the ways,
On ending, do we leave or enter hell?
Our youth's mad dreams spur us, reckless, on;
Such promise waits: a huge uncharted sea!
The eye blinks once and life is wasted, gone,
Leaving love's lost hopes and misery.
Whilst drinking water, I dream of your wine,
And yearn for your soft lips, alluring, sweet,
Their kiss now long denied by envious time:
That thief of all those days when we may meet.
    Away from you an instant seems an age,
      Time has the key, I wait in winter's cage.

LXXVIII

Pale blue is couched on crimson as dying
Day meets night, the eve is filled with stillness
As slowly fades the light, long lingering
My sighing in life's vast wilderness;
Above all else I need your lips respite!
I wander in dark shadow, as evening's sorrow comes,
With the night descending, fatigue's mist clouds my sight,
Then pain recedes as sleep's soft hemlock numbs.
Far off your realm lies open, its rich glades
Tempt inside; there are our dreams unchained,
But your lips softly chide at these charades
And circumstance, by which love is disdained.
    Poor substitute, my dream fills desperate need
     Until your presence sates my aching greed.

LXXIX

Now in the depths of winter I despair:
What point existence eked towards the grave.
Each empty year succeeds each empty year,
Denied those arms, those lips, that touch I crave.
A bargain made remains a bargain made!
Though deep instinct fuels insane desire,
Despite my yearning duty is obeyed!
I turn away for now, will love expire?
I feel its essence in the morning air,
Its presence haunts each evening with the moon.
Each breath sounds love, each heartbeat questions where
Will fate relent and let our love resume?
    A promise binds yet burning eyes compel.
    Love awaits, imprisoned by gates of hell.

LXXX

Why quibble for in mischief's mood
You know that you must win. My logic will refute
Your words, then sultry looks with lids dropped low,
Eyes smouldering, will settle all dispute.
The rational fades as passions blaze:
I peer into those deeps. Such promise lies
Where sense expires, drowned in seduction's gaze.
Thus with your sighs my last resistance dies,
Yet in love's strife your victory brings defeat!
Thus soon you'll get the point my wild coquette.
I'll lead the charge but you will not retreat!
Love's climax ends this conflict, I regret.
    Since Ishtar female wiles have been the cause
      Of men compelled to fight love's endless wars.

LXXXI

Through long lonely nights I lie, tortured
By wild succubi. Red lips tremble with desire,
Dark eyes commanding: *come with me to bed!*
Throw off caution, burn in love's sweet fire!
Hungry, wanton in your greed, vampire nymph
On sex you feed, nipples proud, hips thrust high,
Let your lust inflame my need, writhe you imp:
Fulfil those dreams which waking hours deny.
Nightmare realms thus tantalise, dark and deep
These fantasies; soon the dawn brings such dismay
When I must fret through endless day, for sleep;
For in that realm our sensuous spirits play.
    This incubus his succubus must await,
      At night once more in love drenched Ambergate.

LXXXII

Amid this gentle February rain
I take you in my arms; your kiss is long
And tender-warm, thus vanishes the pain.
For in those endless nights doubts throng
To taunt my fevered brain. Three hours suffice
For me to lose those tortured month's decline
And once again to taste pure paradise;
Thrice love distilled, that rapture, sweet, sublime.
Though we must end this latest tryst, in haste
Soon I must leave; but gladly, love renews.
My heart was not deceived, again I taste
Your burning lips before our soft adieux.
    Meeting, parting, love with fate must vie,
    I steal a kiss before your last goodbye.

LXXXIII

Oh would those eyes with love's soft gaze
Forever here remain, intense and gentle,
Meek and proud, this is the drug I crave,
I'll drink that promise they hold out until
My dying days. Sun and moon and stars look down
In beauty from the skies, the spell they cast
Is deep, sea vast; all lovers in it drown;
I sink enthralled and dream of love just past.
Your unheard music fills my room, your fragrance
Haunts the air, memory plays tricks I swear
Soft shadows hide you there. My dreams enhance
Where breathed romance, still I linger there.
    Love's currents strongly eddy in the mind
    Wild swirls of rapture left for now behind.

LXXXIV

Impulsive! Yes, you always were, in hate,
In all love's moods; yet your forgiving spirit
Wells from springs of pain bequeathed by fate;
And hungering for love because of it.
We came in June to crowded lawns and met
Once more, your dark eyes burned, you chose
Strange words, I knew just what you meant and yet
Was left there ill content. Why? Some cursed god knows.
You stole the gentlest kiss then softly said:
'Let's run away'; a jest I thought, but no!
You froze, and on your distressed face I read:
Dismay: that then I had not wished to go.
    Ten years lost, you faint-heart-fool, love's pain!
    The chance lost there will never come again.

LXXXV

The year meets midsummer and now the long
Decline, though the warm months wait and the corn
Turns gold from green, under lark's sweet song
Where I rest long days at my ease; I mourn.
Deep within my bones I can feel the change,
For the world has turned and sad autumn comes,
With its beauty born of decay, and strange
Restless rage to which my heart succumbs.
All that waits is darkness and unease,
Ennui, sweeping over me like ebb tides,
Leaving love behind, as wreckage, memories
Stranded warped and dry, lost debris of two lives.
    Perhaps love's flame had died as the fruitless years
    Had slipped by? Oh so strong these fears!

LXXXVI

Of six black grapes, two are like your eyes.
A third drips wild juice like your succulent lips,
Another, black velvet skinned, wantonly lies,
The fifth, fleshy, round like your trembling hips,
The sixth signals pleasure at each swollen breast.
The message conveyed as these visions entice:
Of all of love's pleasures those stolen are best;
Although bitter anguish is often their price!
This fruit demands tasting, I think you know why.
Like Adam I'm tempted, I must take a bite,
For natures old urges are hard to deny,
Thus I gorge on lust's banquet long into the night.
    Black grapes now forever remind of a time
      When I found out that love was much sweeter than wine.

LXXXVII

Now heartfelt tears are pouring from the phone
In wrenching sobs you gasp your need for me;
My stomach churns as desperately you moan
For what is lost and now might never be.
Love's tensions grow, heart's fibres take the strain,
Fond hopes die slow, for ruthless time slips by.
Our chance, ungrasped, may never come again,
Cold reason knew what instinct must deny.
But how hard, how hard to tell you no!
My being's very core screamed out: agree!
Choose love, take passion's route, let duty go!
Obey your heart, fulfil your destiny.
    Love bleeds, its fortunes ebbing with the years,
    Past promises dissolving in your tears.

LXXXVIII

Oh, sad November of the dying days
Bleakest month of all with weeping trees;
Corruption falls to wreathe your silent ways,
The stench of dying taints the autumn breeze.
Huddled woods mourn love's deserted grave
Can our joyful days return no more?
With shadows growing darker now I crave
Release from these black months which I abhor.
The light declines and yet I hope you'll wait
Beyond the spectral remnants of this year,
There lingers still that dream of Ambergate.
I think of meetings past, then comes despair.
    Now laid to rest in Autumn's lonely tomb,
      Can spring once more our dying love exhume.

LXXXIX

Soon now comes that saddest season spring
Reminding how we met and all began.
The coming of new light, each waking thing
Recalls when love was new and we were young.
Oh those brooks and banks, your perfume sweet,
The hawthorn blossom white, those evenings late,
Our powerful longing drew us there to meet
Under new love's moon in Ambergate.
There, eye drank wanton eye, lip tasted lip
Lust's burning gale of passion soared and sighed
As we whirled helpless in love's tempest's grip,
Yet by some fault its raging fury died.
    Nothing is left! I wish I could forget,
    The night wind moaning echoes my regret.

XC

Dull aching desperate grey at early dawn
Squeezes the last of dark from cloying night,
A dismal day arrives, its joys stillborn,
Death's world is bathed in melancholic light
And I propelled by that slow engine time
Descend through thoughts of what it is to be,
To drink life's potion, poisoned yet sublime,
Compelled to take love's cup by destiny.
I gnaw existence from declining years
With grim expectance, all dreams turn so ill.
Consoled by this: at least extinction nears,
To cleanse this dross called life of thought and will.
    You gods of chaos why be so unkind
    My world has ended, why leave me behind?

POEMS IN POSTSCRIPT

Carnal Knowledge

A postscript to sundry sonnets

I know that carnal knowledge
With Autumn's corpse must lie.
Putrescence grips
Death bright rose hips
Amid dead columbine.
I would distil love's essence
And suck its breasts, bliss, dry.
Wild nectar drips
Still from your lips
Lush, rich, incarnadine.
Spring's brief faience soon withers
What freshed its glaze must die.
Love's ardour slips,
By years eclipsed,
Hot blood turned thin by time.
Now soon the pen must falter,
My muse you may hear sigh
From yellowed scripts
Where verse depicts
How deep we drank love's wine.

The Silent Queen

I wait until she wakes from slumber
My dark and silent queen of night,
Rich pleasures wait there beyond number,
In her garden of delight.
Sweet, silken, sinful, scents of loving
Lure me to her open door.
Which I would enter, once more proving
Love's red rose can bloom once more.
I **fear** though, will unending darkness
Forever clothe my silent queen?
How long will darkest night possess
My lost forever Proserpine?
I'll wait for Hades gates to open
Releasing love into the light,
Since its bond was anger broken
I live in dark death's dreamed twilight.

To a fellow voyager on a sea of dreams

To a fellow voyager on a sea of dreams,
Did we leave our mark beyond the tides?
Or did we drift like all those pointless lives
And merely service some dark captain's schemes.
Did we rebel and kick against those rules
Which shutter the conformist in his cell?
Or did we bend too readily and well
To play our parts upon this ship of fools.
We two, I think, did mutiny a while,
And crying havoc, left old lives behind;
To try those dangers which wild spirits find
Far up some Orinoco or Blue Nile.
With love and starlight as our only guides
We ventured, not too wisely, but so well
Then yearning's tempests drove our passion's needs
To secret places where raw pleasure bides.
As old Odysseus, safe in harbour now
In Ithaca with comforts won at home,
I feel those longings still and thus would roam
Fresh seas with you at some sleek vessel's prow.

The Regretful Shore

We'll gaze no more across those sands
For life has drifted by.
Though still grey seas must beat those strands
Where once walked you and I.
No doubt our moon delights the bay
Above black waters, deep.
There ceaseless tides forever play
And lover's secrets keep.
There young, joyful, forms must lie
Where we once joined as one,
For hours beneath that starry sky
Where foolish dreams were spun.
It's pointless to regret lost nights,
An ending comes to all.
Affirming life we reached love's heights
And answered well its call;
Which briefly claimed in joy and pain,
What it from all demands,
Till fading visions just remain
Of love's lost golden lands.
We'll gaze no more across the sands,
We join vast nevermore,
And leave our dreams of love's lost lands
On that regretful shore.